Hill Farm
...and the story of Bewdley Plotlands

Tony Harrold

Printed by Print&Digital, Lichfield.
All rights reserved. No part of this publication may be reproduced, stored in a retrieval system, or transmitted in any form or by any means, electronic, mechanical, photocopying, recording or otherwise, without prior permission of the author.
ISBN 978-1-5272-9986-3
EBROOK PRESS

Contents

- **i** Acknowledgements
- **ii** Introduction
- **1.** England Awake
- **2.** Green and Pleasant Land
- **3.** Dark Cloud Rising
- **4.** They Paved Paradise
- **5.** Get Up, Stand Up!
- **6.** Visions of Albion
- **7.** Memories from the Farm
- **8.** Around and About
- **9.** A Different World
- **Postscript.** Up on the Hill

Acknowledgements

Index to photographs. Image numbers:
1,2,3,7,8,10,12,13,14,15,17,20,22,23,24,26,27,28,30,34,37,40,44,51 by Rough Magic Images.
Photographs 5,6,18,19,29,31,32,33. Reproduced with kind permission of Jonathan Meades.
Images 4,9,11,16,21,25,35,36,38,39,41 by Rachel Harrold.
All other photographs were kindly supplied by residents or their families.

Thank you to the committee of Hill Farm Residents Association for their assistance. To The Severn Valley Railway and to Bewdley Civic Society for the many helpful contributions of their members. To Wyre Forest District Council. To the former residents of Hawkbatch that have helped and contributed. Thanks to Stefan Szczelkun for his expertise on plotland matters and his many contacts and helpful advice. To Jonathan Meades for the wonderful Severn Heaven documentary and his continued interest in the preservation of this heritage site. To Nigel Simons and Jo Carnegie for helpful hints, support and ongoing I.T. advice (at all hours). Sorry Nige! To Nigel Taylor for historical accuracies at a time when libraries were closed indefinitely. To Lizi Chambers for magically transforming a print layout into a book format.

Plus, an especially huge thank you to the residents, past and present, of Hill Farm for taking the time to share enough memories to fill a bigger book than this. They also trusted me with invaluable family photos and documents, all accompanied by fascinating conversations of times gone and times yet to come. And a big thank you to Rache for putting up with yet another project.

TH

INTRODUCTION.

By Stefan Szczelkun, artist and author of several books including Plotlands of Shepperton, Energy, Chalet fields of The Gower and Food.

Tony Harrold has produced a gem here. The plotlands phenomena are a barely known wonder of the British countryside. A form of working-class culture more than a hundred years old that has survived and thrived in spite of many adversities. The book you have here is a priceless insight into the hidden history of this form of housing and one that might inspire a new approach to housing in an enlightened future.

Tony first tells us what the plotlands are with many updated and original pieces of research that are a welcome contribution to our knowledge. The local history of Hill Farm plotlands community is then related in detail and enriched with a wonderful oral history.

Hill Farm was one of the first plotland communities to get national profile because of maverick documentarist Jonathan Meades' TV programme 'Severn Heaven', first broadcast in 1990. It has since become a cult classic.

As Tony points out, the UK plotlands are finally getting recognition as something to be cherished and looked after as invaluable heritage. The preservation of the improvisational character of these communities is to be welcomed.

S.Szczelkun.

1. England Awake

Northwood Lane says the sign, a no through road formerly known as Rag Lane. Running for 2 miles following the River Severn upstream before ending abruptly at a five-bar gate. Here the road ends and a rough footpath accompanies the river to the picturesque village of Arley. To one side is the river, a constant flow of water from Bridgnorth and beyond, pouring down from the Welsh mountains through Ironbridge. This side of the river is a regular route for hikers taking in the pleasantries of the Severn Valley, the steam railway, Trimpley Reservoir, and the bridge carrying fresh water in pipelines across the Severn from the Elan Valley on the way to Birmingham. There is little reason to drive along Northwood Lane, it does not really go anywhere. Here, looking away from the river, up the long steep slopes of the bank, past where the railway carves a route through the woods and clearings, there is a different sort of beauty. High on the hill, scattered in ribbons along the contours of the slopes are irregular lines of wooden houses. Each one different to the next. Built by their original occupants and tended carefully by the current inhabitants, this settlement has been here for over a hundred years and is the largest surviving Plotlands site in the West Midlands, probably the largest in England.

The bungalow style homes of Hill Farm were once just one of many such sites along The Severn Valley stretching from Bridgnorth to Stourport. Built at various times from the early 1900's they were termed Plotlands. Brought about by a housing shortage and areas of land that were too difficult to farm economically; a solution evolved. People were encouraged to build their own homes or holiday homes which at the same time gave farmers a much-needed income. In this area alone there are similar, smaller sites at Hawkbatch, Pound Green and Trimpley while many others have now disappeared from elsewhere along the valley or have simply become more regular, traditional style houses. Across England, plotlands sites sprang up free of the restrictions of the later Town and Country Planning Act of 1947. Essex, Surrey, Kent, Sussex, Cheshire, Thames Valley, Merseyside all had plotlands, Wales and Scotland too. Few of these sites remain, although forward thinking councils are now learning to appreciate their history and value, some coining the term "Plotlands Heritage".

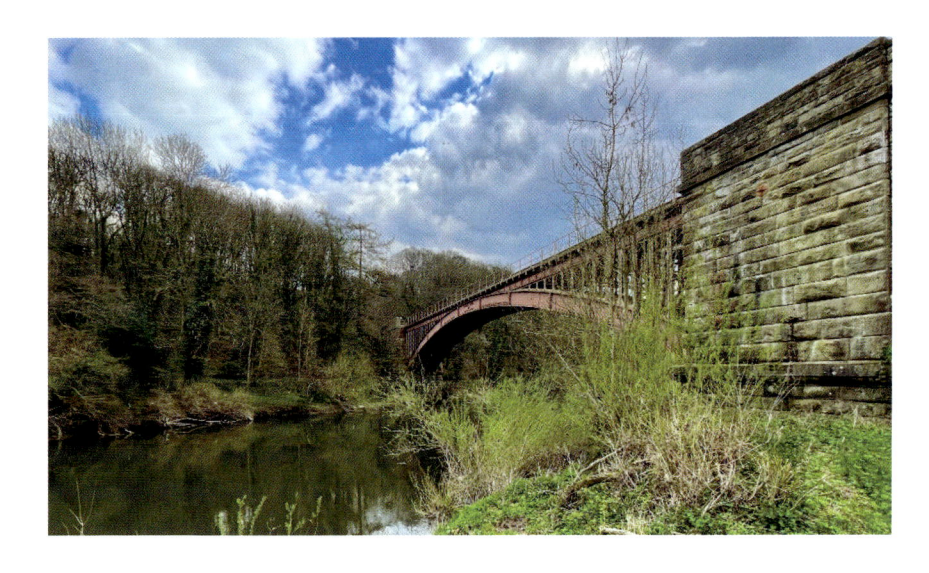

1. *"The inescapable features of the landscape and its story are the railway and the river as they run together through the valley."*

In Langdon, Essex, once the site of a large plotlands colony there is a dedicated Plotland Museum situated in an area of what is now a wildlife conservation site.

In the aftermath of the First World War, with peace restored cheap imports resumed, the price of wheat halved. The Corn Protection Act of 1917 (brought in to safeguard prices and supply during the years that much of the workforce was away fighting), was repealed in 1921. This resulted in farmers losing their governments payments. Cheap grain imports led to many farms going bankrupt. Many farmers' sons did not return from the war. Many of the land workers too. Death duties had doubled. The result of these circumstances was that a quarter of all land in England changed hands during the first decades of the 20th century. Those that were demobilized returned with a dire need for recuperation from injury, gas or shell shock, and a yearning for fresh air. They also returned to a land of food shortages and a lack of decent housing.

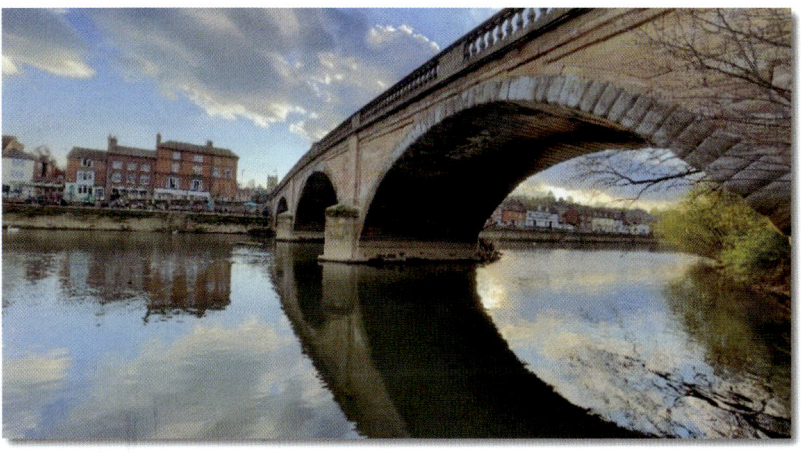

2.

3.

4.

From this period and through the 1930's, the government, aware of the need for slum clearance and new homes, gave encouragement to many new housing initiatives. Huge swathes of countryside on the outskirts of cities and towns were acquired for new municipal housing in the drive to build "Homes for heroes". A creditable project, high on hope but short on finance. As cities and towns burst their boundaries, entrepreneurs bought up bankrupt farms, splitting the plots into smallholdings, some farmers simply offered plots as weekend retreats for those desperate to escape the town. A guinea could buy a year's lease on a small area of a field. A capacity for endurance was the essential factor required for those settling on these sites all over Britain for this was land on the margins. All sites suffered disadvantages: steep inclines, heavy clay soil, windswept, liable to flooding. There were no roads nor mains services. It was Shangri La, but only for those who dared.

5.

The intrepid persevered. Across the land, obsolete railway carriages were being disposed of for as little as £15, often this included transport to site. The potential for an almost perfect retreat. Then began a whole new struggle to get them into place. Farmers assisted with tractors; all willing hands were put to use.

6. A former railway carriage, recycled into a comfortable home.

Surplus ex-Ministry of Defence army huts were in abundance with the added attraction that they were more transportable, and easier to build onto as and when required. Old buses, and even in one known case, a glider body was utilized. Of course, some of these were neither equipped to stand the test of time or the wrath of any local planning inspectors who termed them, "shacks or buildings of less than permanent materials." Over time, these eccentricities evolved into bungalows, differing only from traditional buildings by their wooden exteriors and the individual flourishes of their builder.

7.

Shortly before the Second World War, the 'Holidays with Pay Act 1938' came into force. Suddenly over 18 million people were getting paid holidays, most of them for the first time. Cheap rail trips and charabanc excursions opened the country up to leisure seekers, motorbikes and sidecars were as commonplace as cars. People flocked to the seaside and to beauty spots. The plotlanders having their retreat, now had the opportunity to rent it out to gain the income to finish or improve the build.

8.

9.

10.

Among their number were retirees, weekenders from industry, those seeking solace or recuperation, soldiers, artists and artisans. Some plotland sites became vogueish among theatre and movie icons, particularly those within easy reach of the London railways. Meanwhile in the rest of the country people escaped the cities and towns in search of their own place in the sun. The history of the plotlands continues in one form or another to the present day but its heyday of originality was in those years between the wars.

11.

Rickyard Meadow, Hill Farm 201

2. Green and Pleasant Land

"Seeking fresh air in plotland locations was a sensible move and probably a life saver for many". Plotlands of Shepperton. Stefan Szczelkun.

The plotlands of Hill Farm proved so popular it had its own shop to cater for the community. Better still, it eventually got its own railway station, Northwood Halt. This brought in people from the nearby conurbations of Birmingham and the Black Country. Houses, or shacks as they became derogatorily known by their detractors, sprang up dotted along the farm tracks, lanes and fields. Each facing in the direction the owner deemed to provide the desired view, pleasant meadows separated the rows. Each plot also providing some remuneration for the then impoverished farmers of this beautiful but contrary landscape.

The shortage of materials coupled with the austerity of the inter war years made for some strikingly individual architecture. Without the constraints of architects and planners, hardworking families were limited only by their imagination (and what they could get their hands on). Dwellings were made from wood, asbestos, corrugated iron, ex-Army huts. Railway carriages were given balconies and porches. A disused cricket pavilion in one case was dismantled and brought up to Hill Farm where it was painstakingly reassembled. It still stands now, carefully extended into a pleasant family home. Most cabins were made from pre used and weathered materials. Coach-bolts pinned walls together, floorboards were laid upon railway sleepers, and timbers were sawn to accommodate window frames.

Architecture created by those employed in the 'Workshop of the World', as Birmingham was known. Jonathan Meades described the buildings as "Folk-Art." All were individual and varied homes, normally finished in wood treatments or army surplus paint, brown, khaki or green.

Originally seen as gaudy but because of this use of natural colours and materials, the cabins eventually began to blend with ease into hedgerows of the surrounding farmland. Dismissed as shanties or shacks, over time the garish gave way to a more traditional style bungalow.

"...the irony is that many of those features which have for so long been regarded as offensive are now, as they become more scarce, worthy of conservation." Arcadia for All. Dennis Hardy and Colin Ward.

Site rules, (there were only 3 rules at Hill Farm in those early days), requested bungalows and caravans were to be painted green or brown. Here, among the trees and hedges, they simply became part of nature, allowing human habitation to be incongruous. Nowhere here has anything as indelible as the concrete and steel footprints of urbanisation.

12.

> **RULES FOR HOLIDAY BUNGALOWS AND CARAVANS AT HILL FARM**
>
> 1. All bungalows and caravans must be kept in good repair, and painted brown or green.
> 2. All owners must notify the farm before any change of ownership.
> 3. There is a dump provided and no litter should be dropped in the fields or woods.

13. *Site rules (from approximately 1950's).*

The Hill Farm development evolved to tread very lightly on the Earth. As lightly as the sheep grazing on the meadows between the cabins and the bat colonies that live in some of the roofs. Several of the bungalows have been in constant occupation by the same family for almost 100 years, passed down through generations. Self-built with materials often transported on bikes, buses, trains or carried strapped to motorcycle combinations. Some were used as weekend retreats by the furnace workers, carpenters, engineers, miners and foundrymen of the nearby towns. Babies have been born here, children have grown up in this idyll, workers have retired here, and holidaying relatives have been hosted and entertained.

14.

15.

  The Hill Farm plotlands are a hidden gem, a record of how life was in a time when it was important to use every single last resource, when recycling was a necessity not an afterthought.

The reward for this was a satisfaction beyond monetary value, not one of these dwellings was built with any intention of financial gain. Hill Farm shows what happens when humans apply their skill and endeavor into building their own homes with their own hands. The simple most basic urge to build shelter for family or tribe, an urge since discouraged by those that saw no profit in this.

Hill Farm expresses individualism. It proudly hints at anarchy or the pioneer spirit but settles for a benign, neighbourly, live and let live feel. No static home site ever looks this good or spacious. Rustic innocence by pure mischance. These unique buildings have no place in the handbook of the commercial architect. You do not need a spreadsheet to build a cabin, no mortgage was necessary or even possible. Plotlanders simply built what they could with what they had. Extensions were added as and when money, time and materials became available. Here, those that work the tools to service the upper and middle classes used the same tools to build their own shelter and in doing so bypassed commerce and corporate finance. The result is an ad hoc spa town for the working class, fresh and the opposite of the homogenization of mass suburbia. The cabins live as unobtrusively among the hills as the many trees.

16.

17.

3. Dark Cloud Rising

"The recollection of plotland people is a simple tale of quiet enjoyment without personal gain or pretension." Arcadia for All by Dennis Hardy and Colin Ward.

Not everyone saw the beauty of the movement. All over the country, plotland sites were finding local authorities to be less than sympathetic. In the Home Counties, plotlanders had been sold sites by businessmen who had snapped up huge swathes of land difficult to farm, selling off small parcels as plots. Promises of roads and mains services never came to fruition leaving councils and plot holders with the problem. This was a consequence of businessmen and certainly not due to any failings of the bold individuals that simply sought a better life. Used to living in towns and cities and the deprivation of space, most incomers embraced the clean air and put up with any inconveniences such as unmade roads. But many local authorities now had a different vision for those plotlands that occupied coastal sites or areas of scenic value.

18 and 19. *Severn Heaven.* J. Meades

World War 2 and the aftermath saw areas of the South coast plotlands cleared in the interests of national security. The plotlands of the Thames came under scrutiny, possibly due to the proximity of Windsor and Eton and perhaps the politics of envy.

When a large house is spotted on a headland or high on a hill, people speculate "What a wonderful view they must have!" Somehow, when smaller houses are on scenic hills (and the owner's income is similarly small), they are then deemed to spoil the view. Perhaps as simply as Jonathan Meades states:

"A measure of class hatred." Severn Heaven 1990 Jonathan Meades.

Many of the freehold plotlands faced demise as the land they were built on became worth more than the buildings themselves. The Town and Country Planning Act of 1947 brought an end to any further plotland development although it did not wholly deal with what was already there. In fact, that which was already there had much support both then and now.

"Inevitably (or is it just that our perception has changed?) these are more interesting to the eye than the everywhere-type houses. And if our criterion is to be the degree of unobtrusiveness on the riverside scene, they are, just because of their tiny scale, less noticeable than their newer, larger neighbours." Arcadia for All, Dennis Hardy and Colin Ward.

4. They Paved Paradise

In a fine example of "beware what you wish for", there are few of the original shacks remaining among the cleared plotland coastal areas from Kent heading west through Sussex. The former plotlands at Dungeness, Camber, Peacehaven, Selsey Bill, and Shoreham were replaced by joyless caravan sites, rows of identical bungalows, holiday camps and a couple of nuclear power stations. Although there are a few nature reserves there, there is an irony about the sudden desire for land which no one previously wanted and what it subsequently became.

In Lincolnshire, the 'Humberstone Fitties' plotlands were taken under the wing of the local authority who made the site a conservation zone, preventing unwanted development and ensuring future planning control. This positive relationship with the local authority lasted many years until recently when the council sold a long-term lease of the 'Fitties' to a park-home owner. The original residents (who had raised funds to buy the site themselves) were disappointed and environmentalists dissatisfied with what they see as further spread of the static holiday home with the customary uniformity and the lack of open space.

Elsewhere, the growing population of the Southeast saw London sprawling beyond its boundaries. The Basildon Development Corporation was formed to oversee the formation of a new town. A London/Essex overspill with new houses, roads and industrial areas. This threatened the many plotland communities abounding in South Essex. There were undoubtedly problems attached with these sites, some without main roads and mains services, but there was also much comradery among the residents. Most Essex plotlanders had escaped the overcrowding of London and were in no hurry to rejoin any new urban development. There was huge sympathy for the cause of those to be displaced.

"Any solution which includes the wholesale demolition of substandard dwellings cannot be contemplated. However inadequate, every shack is somebody's home."
Sir Bernard Braine, as quoted from Re-development of Basildon, Town and Country Planning 1973. W.G.Kington.

Eventually Basildon Village gave way to a new town. Plotland communities were swallowed up in the wake with many bought out, offered alternative housing or both. The Countryside Commission created a parkland and tourist attraction with a plotland museum at Langdon. Among the woods, the remains of bungalows hide while one building, 'The Haven', has been restored 1930's style and is now a dedicated plotlands museum.

Meanwhile there are other surviving plotlands. Farndon, Deeside has now become an accepted and positive feature in the landscape. In South Wales, Holtsfield has become a conservation area lauded by the local tourist board.

"Holtsfield- A fascinating insight into an era which is rapidly disappearing." WalesOnline.

The many different locations of the original plotland movement all share commonalities. The descriptions of shacks and shanties, the expression of self-build, the lack of mortgages required, the pioneer spirit and the wave of optimism as both plotlander and farmer combined to improve an unsatisfactory situation. The negatives of the movement came when big business became a middleman, stepping in between (self) builder and farmer then stepping out before fulfilling whatever obligations it had promised. 'The Town and Country Planning Act of 1947' may have stopped any more plotlands, but it has indirectly ensured the preservation of these landscapes as councils came to realise the value of a unique movement.

"…the plotlands are a crucial but now hidden expression of working-class culture." Plotlands of Shepperton 2020, Stefan Szczelkun.

Elsewhere, some former railway carriage houses are recognized as having qualities in their own right. Near Malvern in Worcestershire, Providence Bungalow is now a Grade 2 listed building, consisting of two parallel carriages under a traditional style roof. Swindon Villa in Withiel, Cornwall is another railway carriage build that became Grade 2 listed in 1988. Norfolk also has an example of conservation of carriage conversions.

"In Norfolk, an 1899 Great Eastern carriage, converted into a cottage in the 1930s, was recently donated to the North Norfolk Railway and re-erected at Holt." Fiona Newton, Institute of Historic Building Conservation May 2012

20.

21.

5. Get up, Stand up!

Back on the Worcestershire/Shropshire border, and in particular the River Severn Valley, Worcestershire District Council published a report.

"The term shack is used to describe those buildings constructed of materials of less than average permanency and used for occupation on a full time or holiday basis. The definition is necessarily vague since the structures involved range from elaborate and well-equipped wooden buildings to bizarre conversions of vehicle bodies." Severn Valley Shack Survey 1951.

The report counted and listed these buildings, deciding they should be discouraged or even removed in some cases. Calling them temporary buildings it bemoaned the fact that many were lived in, blaming the wartime bombing for increasing the population of the chalets.

"The origin of many shack sites stems from a housing crisis after the 1914-18 war. Air raids on the West Midlands conurbation led to many evacuees taking up permanent residence and choosing to stay on after the war." Severn Valley Shack Survey 1951.

Of course, in Worcestershire and Shropshire like many other local authorities, the council had readily accepted the rates paid by the bungalows, they just did not like what they saw as the "problem" of them. The lack of any mains infrastructure being one such problem. Worcestershire County Council began a campaign to remove the buildings while reluctantly accepting many cabins were actually quite well-maintained bungalows.

Dear Sir,

Don't let the side down. If you have not already contributed your £2 donation towards the appeal against Worcester County Council orders to remove the bungalows from Hill Farm sites by December, 1964, will you please let the Treasurer - Mr. R. E. Smith, 3, Pratt St., West Bromwich, or your Committee Member have your remittance by return.

But more important still, will you please see that your bungalow is in good repair and decoration and that the site and bungalow are attractive by not later than the 10th September, when members of the County Council will be inspecting the bungalows.

A copy of the minutes of the meeting held on the 24th June is enclosed.

Yours faithfully,

22.Residents Association letter. (1960s)

Town and Country Planning Act, 1947.

ENFORCEMENT NOTICE.

To: Mr.P.H.Finch.   (Occupier of the land hereinafter referred to)

of Forest View, Hill Farm, Bewdley.

WHEREAS it appears to the Worcestershire County Council (hereinafter called "the County Council") that the following development:-

1) the placing of a wooden bungalow.
2) the use of land as a site for the said wooden bungalow.

has been carried out at Hill Farm, Bewdley, without the grant of permission required in that behalf under Part III of the above Act and in contravention of previous planning control within the meaning of Section 75 of the above Act.

AND WHEREAS the County Council consider it expedient to serve this notice on you.

NOW THEREFORE the County Council require you on or before the 30th day of September 1953, to take the following steps for restoring the land to its condition before the development took place, namely :-

(1) remove the said wooden bungalow from the land
(2) cease using the land as a site for the said wooden bungalow

* This notice shall take effect on the 30th day of September 1951.

Dated this 16th

23. *Local council letter sent to residents. (1950s)*

Jonathan Meades, with a quote worthy of being made into a sign which should be placed at the entrance to Hill Farm,

"Officious bureaucratic attempts to have these places demolished come around with dreary regularity." Severn Heaven. Jonathan Meades.

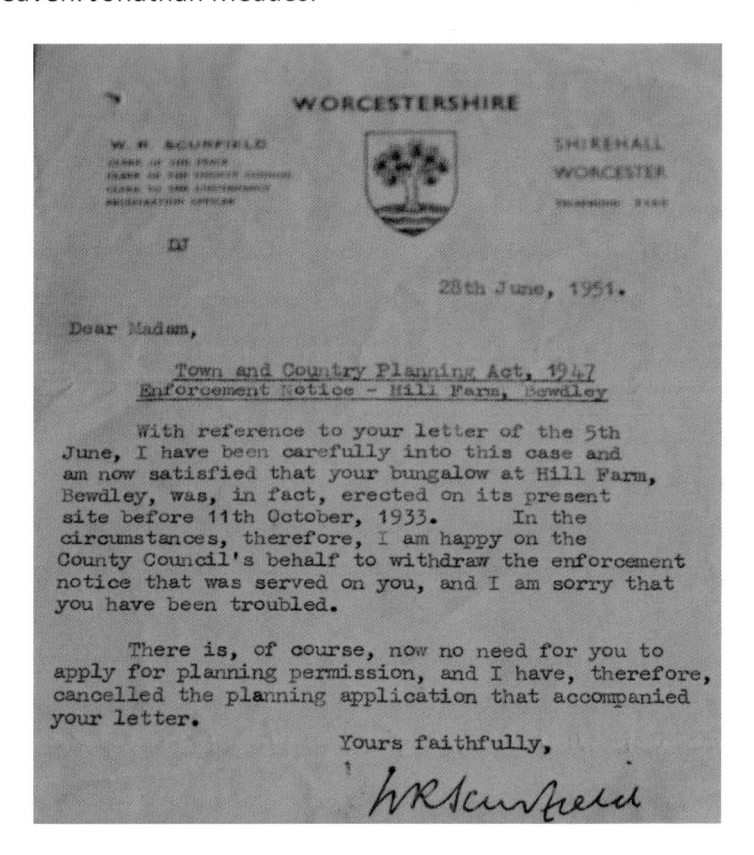

> **WORCESTERSHIRE**
>
> W. R. SCURFIELD
> ...
>
> SHIREHALL
> WORCESTER
>
> 28th June, 1951.
>
> Dear Madam,
>
> **Town and Country Planning Act, 1947**
> **Enforcement Notice – Hill Farm, Bewdley**
>
> With reference to your letter of the 5th June, I have been carefully into this case and am now satisfied that your bungalow at Hill Farm, Bewdley, was, in fact, erected on its present site before 11th October, 1933. In the circumstances, therefore, I am happy on the County Council's behalf to withdraw the enforcement notice that was served on you, and I am sorry that you have been troubled.
>
> There is, of course, now no need for you to apply for planning permission, and I have, therefore, cancelled the planning application that accompanied your letter.
>
> Yours faithfully,
>
> W R Scurfield

24. *Subsequent letter withdrawing threat of removal with an apology, 1951.*

Following the 1947 Act and as a result of the Worcestershire Shack Survey 1951, the County Council sent letters to the owners demanding the removal of their buildings. None of this was an easy task. Some plotlanders had another address, and those that were in occupancy were by nature neither the most communicative, nor particularly respectful of bureaucracy. There was a suspicion of those outsiders with suits, taking photographs and measurements.

The Hill Farm residents banded together to fight the instruction. Resources were pooled into legal representation, and it was pointed out to the council many of the buildings were 'pre 1933 Act' bungalows and therefore did not need planning permission. The council backed down, admitting they would be happy to withdraw the enforcement notice. Hill Farm survived, but in the years that followed, the number of dwellings between Bridgnorth and Stourport declined as some elderly residents did give up the fight and were moved into alternative accommodation.

The purge was renewed in the 1960's with further notices served on many other plotland buildings including both pre, and post 1933 Act Dwellings at Hill Farm, despite the former previously being recognized as legal entities. The council offered several potential solutions to what they saw as a problem. These solutions ranged from compulsory purchase with compensation, to re-housing all owners: even to doing both or doing nothing at all. The residents had to dig deep for legal fees for the battle, they were assisted by their landlord (Farmer and site owner J.A. Halford), who offered to put up half of the funds. This was a timely reminder of the earlier arrangement whereby land that was difficult to farm had previously been allowed to reap an alternative income.

Locally, petitions were signed, shopkeepers and other businesses supported the residents. Sir Keith Joseph, Minister for Housing at the time, over-ruled the planning authority stating many of the structures were outside planning control and would have to be allowed to remain. After hearing arguments that the buildings had been at Hill Farm from as early as 1923 (although in fact, some had been there even longer), and that Kidderminster Rural Council had approved plans as recently as 1946, in 1963 the court ruled in favour of the residents. A decision separately endorsed by this much later summary by the respected architecture critic, Jonathan Meades.

"I find these settlements heartening. They are far more pleasing than most formally planned ones both to look at, and no doubt, to live in." Severn Heaven. Jonathan Meades.

After the battles of the 50's and 60's, slowly the local authorities' attitude towards the plotlands had softened. Worcestershire Countryside Studies (believed to be approx. 1970).

"The bungalows and shacks, with few exceptions are located on sites which with some improvement of facilities and landscaping, could become an acceptable element of the valley."

While a further survey by Worcester County Council (1979) mentioned.

"This site (Hill Farm) has a long and complicated planning history-some of the dwellings have established user rights while others were granted planning permission on appeal in 1963."

In the following years, the local councils of the Wyre Forest area turned the former industrial sites of the valley into a country park. Walking this stretch of river now it is easy to forget the past. Until 1969 there was a large coal mine at Highley. Locally, large quarries provided the very sandstone used to build Worcester cathedral. The Severn Valley Railway, one of the most popular tourist attractions in the Midlands traverses this stretch of river. From historic Bridgnorth, it steams through Worcestershire Country Park at Highley, giving the occasional glimpse of plotland bungalows dotted among the hill and valley, before the train arrives at beautiful Bewdley. Then, after leaving the river the train runs through the West Midlands Safari Park on its way to Kidderminster. The river, meanwhile, courses through towards the historic canal town of Stourport where there were many other plotland bungalows, sadly few of which remain now.

25.*River Severn near Trimpley.*

Summer homes in Severn vale to stay

BIRMINGHAM and Black Country people who have summer homes in the Severn Valley, near Bewdley, have won their right to stay there.

The Minister of Housing, Sir Keith Joseph, today over-ruled the Worcestershire planning authority's decision that the site at Hill Farm, Bewdley, must close next year.

Many of the 231 owners of bungalows and caravans at the farm went to a public enquiry nine months ago to support the owners of the land in their appeal against the planners' decision.

The Minister's inspector was told that it would deprive 1,000 town dwellers of a chance to get into the countryside at weekends.

A petition signed by 414 Bewdley residents and shopkeepers supported them.

NO MORE

The inspector reported that many of the structures were outside planning control and would remain whatever decision was given.

CASH REFUNDS FOR YOU

26. There was much local interest in the resident's battles.

LEGAL FIGHT OVER SEVERN HOLIDAY BUNGALOWS

MIDLAND industrial workers who spend their summer weekends by the Severn in holiday bungalows near Bewdley, packed the Kidderminster Rural Council Chamber today to hear legal argument about their right to stay on the land.

The room which normally seats 24 councillors, officials and reporters, held 70 people when the Ministry of Housing Inspector conducting a public enquiry, asked for the doors to be closed. "I cannot ask for more chairs," he said, "or the Council will have to send home some of its staff."

A dozen of the bungalow tenants who could not get in listened through open windows.

The owners of Hill Farm, Northwood Lane, Bewdley, the executors of the late Mr. A. E. Halford, are appealing against refusal by Worcestershire County Council of planning permission for use of the farm for bungalows and caravans, some of which are now their owners' only homes.

Mr. Guy Seward, for the owners of the 264-acre farm and the tenants, said the earliest of the 234 buildings on the land was erected in 1923. The Planning Authority had agreed that 85 of them were there before control was imposed and could remain.

NOT CONFIRMED

Plans for the site were approved by the Rural Council in 1946, Mr. Seward said, but had not been confirmed by the Kidderminster Joint Planning Committee when that Committee was dissolved by the 1947 Planning Act.

Mr J. D. Schooling, for the County Council, said enforcement notices served on the land owners in 1951 and 1952 had not been challenged and the time limit for the use of the land had expired at the end of last year.

27.

WESTON, FISHER & WESTON,
SOLICITORS,
COMMISSIONERS FOR OATHS

G. NEVILLE WESTON,
T. E. LALONDE

G. N. Weston

26, Vicar Street,
Kidderminster

GNW/DW

18th September 19..

Re: Hill Farm Bungalow - No. 174.

    We now return the letter received by you from the Worcester County Council establishing the permanent nature of the bungalow owned by you at the Hill Farm and are obliged for the use of this at the Enquiry.

                  Yours faithfully,

Enc.

28. *A long and complicated planning history.*

6. Visions of Albion

29.

Going back to 1902, Hill Farm was simply a small part of the huge Bewdley estate of almost 2,000 acres, sold in lots at auction by Grimley and Sons of Temple St. Birmingham. Along with Hawkbatch Farm and Cottage, Dowles Farm, Northwood Farm, Dowles Manor House and many other farms local to Bewdley, this estate was the inheritance of Beatrice Mary Wallop, nee Pease, and by that time Countess of Portsmouth.

The Pease family were wealthy industrialists with interests in transport, coal, minerals and banking.

30.

They were also Quakers and campaigned against slavery and animal cruelty. Beatrice Mary had been born to Edward Pease and Sarah Sturge (of Bewdley). Edward later founded both Darlington Library and The Society for Suppression of the Opium Trade, he was part of a large Quaker family involved in politics, industry and philanthropy. Ill health forced Edward to leave the family business. Moving to Bewdley, he concentrated on horse breeding. Edward Pease died in 1880, his wife Sarah preceded him in 1877, and so young Beatrice Mary was brought up by her uncle, Joseph W Pease with his wife and their own large family.

In 1885 Beatrice Mary Pease married Newton Wallop, the Sixth Earl of Portsmouth also known as Viscount Lymington. Beatrice Mary took the title of Countess of Portsmouth in 1891.

In a story deserving a book of its own: apparently to raise funds for the Earl and his political career, and against the advice of Joseph W. Pease, the Earl and Countess instructed the Bewdley estate go to auction. This resulted in a legal battle over mismanagement of the estate whereby the countess successfully sued her uncle leading to the collapse of the Pease family bank. JW Pease died shortly afterwards. Following the ownership by the countess, Albert Edward Halford became the tenant farmer at Hill Farm and the eventual owner of the freehold by the early 1920's.

Due to the nature of temporary buildings, it is impossible to ascertain when the first ones appeared, but I have been told by members of the Halford family, there were already "a couple" on the land when A E Halford took on the tenancy and thus before 1908. Fishermen were welcomed to camp on the meadows and in course, plots were rented out. It was on the lower meadow by the river that there were reports of railway carriages, gypsy caravans and ex-army huts in use as retreats. Wooden bungalows were already a feature of the river landscape around Bewdley and in a continuation of this build it yourself theme, there began a minor urban escape as Black Country folk went back to nature.

The Hill Farm plotlands are spread across one steep bank of the river both above and below The Severn Valley Railway. From Northwood Lane you begin to see some of the bungalows in a meadow at just above river level. Spaciously placed by the riverbank along the same field in two random, but parallel lines, some have been rebuilt into large and luxurious retreats while others retain the original charm of an earlier age. Many are raised high on pillars indicating there are times when the river is prone to burst the banks. This is where in the early days, fishermen pitched their tents and settled down for the weekend's sport.

To enter the meadow, you pass an elaborate wooden shelter covering a noticeboard indicating the names and positions of the cabins. There is a rough map, though not entirely accurate, some of the cabins appear to have identical names, some have names that are similar, and some are placed in the wrong sequence. In the dark winter evenings this must be a delivery driver's nightmare. The wooden framed noticeboard indicates that the fields are under the care of the Albert Halford Trust. The Halfords farmed this land, with its inhabitants, for over 100 years. Steep hills, water flowing down into the roaring river, the heavy clay; all went to make the economics of upland farming grim; these were perfect plotlands.

31.

Mr. Halford and his family would have felt pleased with this new steady, reliable income, free from whatever uncertainties the British weather might bring to their crops or animals.

Welcoming they certainly were. It is widely accepted that cabins were built here from the end of World War One (with anecdotally, one or two pre-dating that time), the Halfords happy to assist with their tractor when required. Residents spoke of being vetted at the farmhouse, of being able to buy rabbits, pheasants, and eggs. Fishing rights were granted with some of the plots for the area of the river north of what is known locally as the "Water Bridge", the pipeline from the Elan Valley that provides water for the Birmingham area. This lower field has come to be known as Severn Meadow with some of the buildings taking their address as Northwood Lane. The lane itself had its share of wooden built bungalows, as did the river track to Bewdley, most of which are gone with some rebuilt in brick. The (then) Worcestershire County Council report for Bewdley refers to 'shacks and dwellings' on both sides of the river both here and going right into the town itself.

Continuing up the narrow lane, but turning uphill there is a railway crossing, ungated since at least two serious accidents years ago. The crossing is now fitted with warning lights and a cattle grid. This is Northwood Halt. Opened in 1935 specially to deal with the influx of people, the station was closed in 1963 before being re-opened by the Severn Valley Railway in 1974. It has been in operation ever since. Northwood Halt had previously fallen into disrepair, now it has been carefully renovated in period style. New signage has been provided and a shelter built to replicate a similar one that was formerly at Foley Halt,

Kidderminster. A plaque tells us this pagoda style shelter was erected by The Friends of Kidderminster Town Station.

Opposite the Halt is Crossing Cottage, once the tied dwelling for farm labourers behind which was a well with its pump from the days when water needed to be fetched by those occupying the land. Before the water pump was there, a nearby stream was the source of fresh water for the hardy visitor. This steep narrow lane is the entrance to the next part of Hill Farm.

Climbing the hill after crossing the railway line the slope steepens. Bungalows appear to the left and right built discreetly into the sides of the hill among the tall trees. The remains of a steep flight of steps carved down the incline are remnants of the days before roads were cut to make access easier. Amidst a clearing, pleasant wooden bungalows continue straight ahead and to the right. Open fields separate the rows and sheep graze contentedly on the grass growing on the hard clay that forms the huge bank running down to the river. One glance at the steep, stony terrain is all that is required to imagine the problems that came with farming this ground. As recently as 2007, not for the first time, rain washed away a large part of the land sending gardens from some plots hurtling down across the railway and beyond.

32.

33.

TELEPHONE 402123

A. E. HALFORD & SON

Hill Farm, Bewdley.

M_____   19

Ground rent for 31st March - 30th September 1975
Inclusive

Fishing at Folly Point approx   22 00
350 yds upstream from water   2 00
bridge. Fishing between   24 00
bungalows approx 130 yds down-
stream from water bridge.

1) All rents must be paid
   before 25th March 1975.

2) A credit charge of 10%
   may be deducted if payment
   is made within 28 days of
   invoice.

34. *A ground rent invoice which included fishing rights for the Severn.*

The bungalows just above and below this first ascent are among the original plots on the farm as you leave the river. Many are still occupied by the same families that originally built the cabin. All tell of a pioneer spirit, a comradery and willingness to help. Some joke that their neighbour's cabin is better built as the collective know-how improved. All over the farm the bungalows are set like hedges around the edges of each field and every meadow is higher up than the one before. Nearly all gardens are carefully tended, buildings have a Wild West frontier look. Milk churns and gas cylinders with carefully carved openings become imaginative letterboxes and individual flourishes abound. Each plot, its stories, its memories, carefully built with more care than could ever have been put into a traditional street or cul de sac. Still surviving in one form or another after almost 100 years. They have weathered well for what were once described as "buildings made of less than permanent materials".

"The day cannot be far off when moves are made to have some of these structures listed". Severn Heaven. Jonathan Meades.

35. *A local character.*

36. *The Severn Valley Railway, Arley Station.*

7. Voices from the Farm

Some contributions from residents, past or present. Some contributors preferred me to use just their initials or first names.

LS

"There were Prisoners of War that worked at the farm during WW2. I remember Ernst and Kurt, Germans. They lived in a chicken pen at first but later moved into the house. Ernst was only about 18 or 19 when he was captured and spoke exceptionally good English. He acted as the interpreter. Ernst stayed in touch with the Halford family, he even sent his 3 children, 2 boys and a girl, to stay for the summer holidays to improve their English. He had a wonderful sense of humour. On his last visit we all took him to the Cock and Magpie for fish and chips."

MJH

"As I have been told, the farm was under the Halford family from around 1908, after taking over as tenant farmers. I believe there were a few buildings already there back in 1908. By the early 1920's the Halfords had become owners of the farm and thus have completed over 100 years on this land. Many people came to camp on here, there were two tons of straw put aside in the barn for the campers to take and bed down on. Special excursion trains would bring them down from the Black Country, fisherman, families, kids and once they were there, they could get cigarettes and provisions from the farm shop. Everything they needed, really.

I remember Kirk and Ernst, 2 German prisoners of war staying, they stayed for a year or so after the war, when I was a child, they made me a wooden horse and cart. The council got a bit revved up in the 60's and there was a bit of a tussle over planning. The residents and AJ Halford worked together with the council and resolved the issues."

R and P
P. "I always wanted to live here; my sister was up on the next field until she died the other year. It is a great community, whenever people go into Bewdley they will always ask if you need anything."
R. "Before we moved in, I was working in Brum and coming down every weekend to try and decorate the place. Each Friday I would fill the car with tools and paint and drive down. I'd open a beer and look at that view, next thing and before I knew it, I'd be driving back to Birmingham on Sunday evening, boot unopened, paint and everything still in there and no work done!"

A
"Our original roof leaked, we got planning permission and bought the stuff for a new one, but we had bats in the loft. In the end we could not disturb them, so we strengthened the lower timbers and put the new roof right over the old one. The bats have been here longer than us, it is their home too."

L
"When we changed our roof, we found it was made from old army ammunition boxes."

T and R
"Our cabin is almost original, although old it was one of those that was not granted approval until the 1962/3 court hearings. The central area is the oldest part with those large oak pillars supporting the roof ridge, it was extended to the side and rear later. The previous owners were here 18 years. They wanted to stay but ill health to a family member meant they needed to move closer to Brum. Before them it was owned by a family that loved the rural lifestyle. They embraced hippy ideologies, putting in a stargazing platform, and decking to view the night skies. They also, fortunately, put in a bypass pipe that carries the stormwater from the top field down past our cabin and away."

P and M
"In the old days, all the men would go out on the field with shovels, dig holes and bury the nightsoil, different spot every week. That was before we had the septic tanks fitted. There were skips by the phone box on the lane for rubbish. I helped rebuild that one (pointing to a bungalow in the middle distance), and that one; that one too, quite a few over the years. You see that new looking one there? Well, it is only part new. We all carried the old building from there, in sections down the bottom there and it is their extension now. See that one over there? It has got our old front door and our old windows.
See that big one up the track? The reason it is that big? There was a railway carriage there originally, family had lived there

since the '50s, they were worried they wouldn't have kept the permission if they moved it, so they just built the new one around the carriage. They lived in the end part for a while until they had cut the carriage up with oxy acetylene and snips and took it out bit by bit. You cannot do that anymore; you need proper plans passed these days. I do remember (laughing), they kept all the glass though."

M

"We lived here for 20 years before we retired, bought the motorhome and went around Europe. Our daughter is here now with her family, she grew up here and has always been in this community. We only stay when we are back in England, even then we are mostly visiting friends or meeting up in The Great Western pub. I don't see us ever living in a brick and tiles house after this long."

T

"I didn't want the bungalow at first. My wife had heard it was for sale, visited and fell totally in love with Hill Farm. She had been down there a number of times before I even went to look. When I did visit, I loved the home-made vibe of the buildings, some of the craftsmanship was amazing. I was concerned about the security of the contract. We went to see Dave and Rose (The Halfords, the farmers), When I asked him about the security of the lease, Dave said, "I know it's unusual, it's just the way it is and has always been, people have been here since the 1920's and passed it down through families". An hour later we had bought the place and have never regretted it."

P

"There are two reasons for living here. You either love the lifestyle or you can't afford anywhere else. We are both of those! It is the big sky, not a light anywhere, you can see eternity from here.
Some move up here thinking they are in the suburbs! They moan about the unmade roads and no lights, the animals, the narrow lane. They never last too long before they move somewhere else."

Stanley

"My family have connections going way back. My uncle was a fisherman and owned a fisherman's shack. This one and many others needed a rebuild back in the '60s due to containing asbestos. The fisherman's train used to bring in loads of people to the Halt on a Sunday."

37.

38 and 39.

54

J.
"I grew up in a bungalow on Northwood Lane, we would buy fresh milk from the farm. Turkeys roamed free by the railway and the weekend all the Black Country kids hung around by the crossing to open the gates for a penny a time and be picking all the mushrooms and blackberries. We moved away but when I got married, we bought a bungalow on Hill Farm. I will never live anywhere else."

Brian and Janet
Janet: "I am one of a big family from Brum, and we'd come here camping. My sister is 94 now and remembers being brought here on the back of a lorry with tents and hay for sleeping on. That would be about 1931. My mom wanted a plot and a man at work said there was a boat and a caravan for sale on Hawkbatch. She bought the caravan, did not fancy the boat, then heard there was a plot going over the river at Hill Farm, there was a shop there so that clinched it. There was an old charabanc on the plot, so she bought it with her sister. We've been connected with here since the 1930's. Then we moved up to this spot and my sister had the plot next door."
Brian: "Yes, her sister was next door and just there was my mom and dad's plot. Up the hill there was my nephew's and down the bottom was my sister as well. My son has that one along here. We also have relatives down the bottom of the hill."

8. Around and About

I received the following comments after a series of requests I made locally for any reminisces about the local plotland areas. With libraries and local authority offices closed due to the pandemic situation, research was difficult, but Worcestershire locals came to the rescue with some heartwarming stories. Some arrived by email, some by phone and some were the results of enjoyable meetings in Bewdley pubs and chance encounters as a result.

Cynthia Pearson
"I was born in 1938 in Blackheath in the Black Country and as a child of 7 I was extremely ill with pneumonia. It was at the end of the war; my recovery was slow and medication scarce at that time. My mother was offered the chance to take me to Bewdley to recover. We spent the 6 weeks holiday at a friend's bungalow on Hill Farm.

As I remember it, the bungalows were arranged around a large field with picket fences surrounding each plot. The building was extremely basic and quite primitive. I know there was a tap in the field where we had to go with a large enamel jug to get water and we had a shed behind the bungalow with an Elsan toilet.

Our delight, as town children, was to pick the mushrooms that appeared in the field and the blackberries from the hedgerow. I remember once my sister was chased by a large pig, and we were all very afraid.

Anyway, I recovered and thrived, I have 2 children and 4 grandchildren. The experience left me with such fond memories of Bewdley I have now lived in the town since the 1990's."

Liz Fudge
"I grew up on Northwood Lane and the fields of Hill Farm were my playground. It was the days when children were free and safe to roam wherever as long as they turned up for tea at the right time. My friend and I spent a lot of time in the field by the river as we were befriended by the owners of one of the buildings there and they provided us with lemonade and cake. They were two very kindly ladies we knew as the Miss Parrys, they lived there with their father who we never met as we never went inside the bungalow. They did not have running water so as repayment we would fill their containers with water from the communal well on the lane. They were happy days, we played among the bungalows, some were little used, some were run down, some were loved. One was an old railway carriage.

My late mother lived in Northwood Lane for 90 of her 92 years and well-remembered the milk deliveries by horse and cart from the Halfords at Hill Farm. She was born in one of the bungalows along the river by the rowing club and moved to Northwood Lane when she was 2. Our family home was a simple bungalow very similar to those on Hill Farm, it was classified as a temporary dwelling. There were many along the river.

My late father also lived along the lane before marrying mum. What a pity we can't ask them for their stories!"

Roger
"I was born in West Bromwich and remember my parents telling me of neighbours who built a bungalow at Bewdley with materials they transported on the bus."

Brian
"There were shacks along Dowles Brook below Knowles Mill on the land that is Worcestershire Wildlife reserve. They have sadly, long gone. I remember railway wagons there. Jonathon Meades described the ones at Hill Farm as 'folk architecture'. They are quite beautiful."

'Gypsy' Joseph
"We used to play up there (Hill Farm) when we were little and visiting relatives. We loved the horses, the sweets from the shop, we used to ask for 'the luck' and it was never denied. There is a lot of magic around there if you know where to look. Yes! They are part of that land up there, living it, they built those homes themselves and there has been a curse on anyone trying to take them away. I have not been round there for years, but they were great days. I am glad to tell you, The Cowboy Angel rides!"

Trevor
"I remember the shacks along the river, they were here and there right down to Stourport and up-river. Only the council called them that as they did not like the random nature of the buildings. The owners called them bungalows and that is what they were. Many were built after World War One by some of the heroes, shell shocked, wounded and gassed on the Somme. They

later became a refuge from the bombing of the industrial areas in World War Two. Lots of owners did not go back after the war, they loved the river and the fresh air. Hill Farm and Hawkbatch have the most, although these days they are a lot more luxurious than they used to be. They are beautiful, built with love and care. I am glad these have survived, so much of our history has vanished. We are lucky to have these as part of our rich local heritage along with the river, the town, the railway and the old quay. This stretch of the river is an incredibly special place."

Joyce Coombs

"My father was a hiker and often walked along the river by the pipeline bridge. One day he saw the farmer at Hawkbatch and asked permission to buy a cabin there. There was a plot going and originally, he built a weekend bungalow. There were several plots on which ex-army huts had been erected as the main part of the building with outside Elsan toilets which were in turn replaced by proper cesspits. Eventually they became quite wonderful bungalows. I have a friend who was born there, I remember so many happy times.

At Hawkbatch there were the cherry harvests. On a Sunday morning everyone would gather around the canning shed and a service would be held. There would be a marquee, harmonicas and squeezeboxes playing with a fete and games on the greens. It was a terrific community.

40.

41. *"Winters can be brutal up here".*

9. A Different World

Rob and Theresa

Rob: "This bungalow was built properly; from level foundations, in sections, and is still on the original footprint. I have documents all the way back to 1942 when my great Grandmother bought the place. The council describe it as a pre-1933 Act bungalow. Most think this community started when the (Northwood Halt) station was built but this and many other bungalows predate that. My family bought it from a Mr. Toll, a baker whose wife had TB. He built it for her to live in the clean air. I have the letter of sale, typed out but finished off in handwriting with the explanation, "I am now too weak to type". Hard days, tough times.

My great gran lived here from 1942 until she died, she is buried over at the Wribbenhall church graveyard. I have been coming here since I was 6 weeks old. My mom would bring me down to visit Nan, we would get the train at Langley Green or Smethwick West and get off at Northwood. When that station closed, we would get off at Bewdley and walk, then that closed, and we'd get off at Kiddy then get the bus to Bewdley. We seemed to be getting further away! My mom had an agreement with a lady at the end of Northwood Lane where she kept a pushchair so she could wheel my sister and me the rest of the way. As I got older, I would play with the kids from the farm, David and Michael, they were a bit older than me. We would go shooting, they would have shotguns, and I had my air rifle. Nan would sit up at the kitchen at the farmhouse with Margaret (Halford). Margaret often gave her a rabbit or a pheasant. I would help with the milking. They would send the bull out; the cows would fall in behind and all would be led back up to the milking shed.

My Grandad was a bit of a character. He would keep chickens here and once had a goat. He bought it back from Comberton Hill on the train. The guard wouldn't allow the goat in the guard's van with him, so he made him take it in the empty first-class compartment."

Theresa: "I was born in Bewdley. My mom worked for Styles, the animal feed suppliers, so she knew the Halfords and the farm quite well. My cousin and myself would cycle along the river to Bridgnorth. We would go along part of Northwood Lane, but I never took any notice of the wooden bungalows, they didn't seem different to any other houses to me. In fact, my Godfather lived in a wooden bungalow on the lane."

Rob: "I used to cycle down here from Oldbury in the Black Country when I was a kid. You know the Raleigh factory there? It backed onto the canal at Oldbury/Smethwick where there was a barge for all the scrap. All the kids would take parts for their bikes, so I built a bike from that barge. I would have been about 11 or 12. In the 6 weeks holiday I would cycle down here straight after finishing school. I would collect my Tilley Lamp and go fishing straight away. I would have the place to myself back then for all but a week or so when some family members turned up for their annual holiday. Then I would just take my tent up into the woods. You could go night fishing without fear of anyone bothering you and I used to walk up to the Pipeline Bridge and fish from there."

Theresa: "When we first met, Rob brought me to see the bungalow. I was shocked when I saw what was in it, or what was not in it! There was a chemical toilet, a gas lamp, a Tilley lamp. Electricity was available but we didn't have it, although we had the pole outside. We did the place up and moved in in the 80's. We had the chemical toilet, then had a cesspit built, now we are on the mains pipe, we also got electricity connected. Our kids were brought up here, playing out the front. The road out there was just a track then and they played in the trees and bushes without fear of cars."

Ray

"I have been here since 1946, I grew up over there (Ferndale), till I was 18. Then I got married, we lived in Bewdley a while and came back to this bungalow at Hill Farm where we are now. I have always been around the railway; always felt I am a part of the 'railway family'. The train ran through the valley right by our bungalow, we would open the crossing gates for the cars and get pennies. We would go to school on the train, the drivers were all Worcester men we knew them by name, they would give us cakes and sandwiches!

42. *A young Ray with his friends*

I would be in bed on a school morning and hear the train going up the line that was my alarm clock, I would get up and catch it to school on its way back to Bewdley. Then when I started work, no surprise, it was for the railway. Now we live just above the same railway line. The Halt was a wooden shelter with a second hut there as a temporary booking office for the busy Sundays. On a weekend morning the fishermen's train would arrive and on Sunday evenings the Halt was packed as trains would take many back to the Black Country and Birmingham.

  We would play in the woods, I broke my arm falling out of one of the trees, trying to copy the squirrels. A neighbour took me to the hospital next morning on his motorbike, me hanging off the back with a broken arm! We would carry sacks to get firewood from the woods and supplies from the garage at the end of the (Northwood) Lane. Gas mantles, paraffin and the like. It was run by Arthur Hoare, he had a big sign at the back, it said "You wreck 'em, we fetch 'em."

43. *Ray and pals on the water bridge.*

"We wore wellies all the time. In the big freeze of 1963, we would get our water from the stream as our tank was frozen. Hands chapped from the cold and legs chapped from the wellies. I'd get water for the (then) people at Pips Villa, and they would always reward me with white chocolate. It was much later I learned that chocolate is normally brown, who knows how old that stuff must have been?

We learned not to use the stream after a storm. There was a well at the back of Crossing Cottage, you had to pump the handle to prime it and get the water flowing.

Mr. Bassett, the postman, lived in the railway carriage on Severn Meadow. He organized cricket and the bonfire night gathering. Herbert, lived up there, he ran the rowing boats in Bewdley so we could go out on the boats any time we liked. Arthur W lived at the top there. He would have to walk up that hill every time to get to his cabin, that's why he called it Dunroamin'. He had a motorbike and sidecar combo and drove to the Jewellery Quarter (Birmingham) every day for work. It was a great community, I remember my friends having a generator and the first telly on here, we would all go round to watch it.

There were some interesting buildings; the railway carriages, gypsy caravans, one bungalow was built around the back end of a charabanc, as well as all the beautiful bungalows. There was talk about making the whole farm a conservation area, some time ago but it did not happen for some reason or other."

44. View from Road Meadow.

45. Note improvised gates made from copper piping.

Glenda

"Our grandfather built the bungalow in the 1920's originally to get the children out of the living conditions of their house in the back to backs in the centre of Birmingham. The lease on my grandmother's shop in Brum was expiring so they transported it, bit by bit, and rebuilt it at Hill Farm. I have heard tales of them on my grandfather's motorbike and sidecar, Nan on the back, kids in the sidecar buried beneath supplies.

In the 50's we had an old army tent which would be erected when needed for the visit of family members who came down on the steam train from Birmingham. I remember looking forward to the tinned fruit and cakes they brought with them. There was no electricity then, but my mother and Grandmother would cook up delicious meals on the calor gas cooker.

The cooker was still working up to recently when it got thrown out when the kitchen was renovated.

There was a Tilley lamp in the living room and evenings were spent together listening to the wireless and playing cards in front of the log fire. I loved reading in bed by candlelight.

Food was bought from Margaret or Joan at the farm. My job was to scald out the milk cans and fetch the milk, often still warm from the cows. Sometimes it tasted of the wild garlic that the cows had been eating in the meadows.

Water was brought from the tap up the field and carried on our trolley cart. We never wasted water. We had an outside toilet and washbasin with flushing water fed by the tank of rainwater from the roof. Friends came to marvel at our modern toilet!

I also remember we had fishing rights on the Severn. I remember fishing for tiddlers using my mother's old stockings. I'd bring them back to the bungalow, keeping them in an old Belfast sink in the garden and feed them on the ant eggs we'd dig out of the molehills. We would wonder freely for miles in any direction, picking mushrooms and scrumping apples from the orchard. I loved milking times, we played in the barn when it was raining although that stopped when the barn burned down.

46.

47. *A young Glenda*

In the 50's and 60's not many residents had cars. My mother and I would start walking down the lane to Bewdley, but we never had to walk far, someone would always stop their car and offer us a lift. A different world!

People were very inventive. In the 50's I remember the gates were no longer animal proof. My grandmother got mad when the sheep got in and ate her vegetable crop- or even worse, her montbretia! My father was a plumber and all he had to hand were some lengths of pipe, so he used them to make new gates. My mother was not at all pleased with their appearance, but they did keep the animals out though. They are still there to this day.

Various family members have lived in the bungalow. Now we are up to six generations of us that have enjoyed the peace and quiet."

48.

Graham

"My Grandad built our bungalow in 1928. He looked at the river field first, there were already a few buildings down there. I remember railway carriages with porches, but he decided on higher ground. It is one of the first five on this field. That was before there was any water supply, even before the standpipes. I was told they fetched water from the stream down past the crossing and boiled it. His was finished first on this field, they all pitched in and helped each other with the buildings. He always joked the others had better bungalows as they had ironed out any mistakes by then!

There were loads of kids up here among the cows, sheep and horses. There were pig sties over the far field. You know about the shop? We would all go up there to spend our pennies we earned opening the crossing gates. There were quite a few that were living at the farm then, extended family. They told us that is not the original farm building, the earlier one was really small, I think it became used to house pigs after the newer house was built. I was told prisoners of war came here to work, some of them even came back for a holiday long afterwards. We would walk along the river to Bewdley, there were quite few wooden bungalows there. They have all gone now or been replaced in brick. I eventually took over our bungalow, there are still lots of original features, but the view has changed. I can tell because you can see the river in our old photos, now trees and hedges have grown all around."

49. *A young Graham at the crossing*

50. *Forest View, approx. 1960s*

Jane

"When I was a child growing up here, we had lots of community events, Easter egg hunts and every year we had a bonfire in my field. They would all put a few coppers in to buy fireworks, we would have potatoes in the bonfire, chestnuts, sweets, our penny for the guy campaign would help.

Mr. Garratt would go into town every morning to fetch newspapers for all who wanted them. We bought eggs, rabbits and milk from the shop and my dad always bought a turkey from the Halfords for the school at Christmas.

All the kids on the site used to go and sit with Margaret Halford and help her bottle feed the orphaned lambs, there were nearly always goslings in the front garden and chickens with their chicks running around.

We played in the hay barns and scrumped apples and plums from the orchard. We walked the back fields mushrooming on Sunday mornings as Sunday was always big breakfast day.

Everyone was auntie or uncle. Uncle Jack up at the Old Wagon Wheels had a very cheeky mynah bird that we used to wind up and get to swear.

If anyone was repairing, extending or re-building, everyone helped. My dad's electrician from his business used to have a place here too, Bertie Belmore. He had a small fire at his bungalow and all of us kids were sent round with buckets, sponges, cloths and polish to help him to clear up. So many happy memories of this community."

Von

"My Grandparents, Alfred and Elsie Collett, used to rent a cottage on Northwood Lane for a week in the summer in the 1940's. They grew to love Bewdley, although getting there from Smethwick was a trial. They used to walk around Hill Farm, often passing a plot where an old gypsy caravan had stood empty for years. One day they were chatting to the farmer, he said they could take on the plot. So, over 70 years ago, in 1948 the Collett history at Hill Farm began.

My Grandfather had the gypsy wagon towed off and replaced with an ex-military dental railway carriage he found for sale at the Ford dealership in West Bromwich. He arranged transport and my dad and uncle, as teenagers, went along for the ride. Things did not go quite to plan though as the lorry could not get up the hill at the railway crossing and the driver left the carriage on the lane. My grandparents enlisted the help of farmer (John?) Halford who pulled the carriage up the hill with the tractor. It was put into place and the plot re-named Al-Ron, after my father and my uncle, Alan and Ron.

Over the following years they added sheds and a toilet. My Nan had a beautiful rose garden, I do not know how she got them to grow in that clay. They had many friends there including their neighbours, Harry and Alice Lucas who owned Royston, and Alf and Elsie Teales from Des Res, all originally from Smethwick.

The dental carriage lasted well but was eventually replaced around 1957. My parents and my aunt's family took the place on, we continued to spend happy summers up at the farm. Over the years my family continued to extend and modernise, and Al Ron was passed down through the family again. Today we have all mod cons, a beautiful garden and best of all, indoor plumbing!"

John and Sylv

"I have been coming up here since I was 2 years old. We would get 3 buses, Wednesbury to Dudley, Dudley to Kidderminster, Kiddy to Bewdley and then we would walk the 2 miles down the lane and up the hill. Me on my dad's shoulders hanging on, he only had one arm, he had lost the other in the (First World) war. There were old railway carriages in the bottom field, but we camped further up the hill around the sides of the fields. There have been people on Hill Farm since before the 1920's, I have heard before that even, possibly from before the Great War."

51.

52.

"Margaret (farmer's wife and site owner), used to come around every day, checking everyone. Someone had brought an old fowl pen to sleep in and I remember lots of tents for the fishermen. As kids, we would all sleep in the barn, on the hay. My Uncle (Ray Vaughan) built Hilary in 1937, it was the smallest one back then and known as the 'Doll's House'. The woodwork was beautiful, he was a master craftsman. In later years it was extended. There were already quite a few cabins then. When we came to stay, we would go and get the water from the standpipes by the field in a white enamel jug, the water shone crystal clear against the enamel as it poured. I remember as a kid I would run around the field collecting eggs, the hens laid them all over the fields. I used to collect them all and take them up to the farmhouse. Until I told me mum. She told me collect some and bring them to her!

We have had three cabins over the years and brought our kids up here. We have photos of them playing with the horses, there were pigs as well and the old rope swing on the tree. It is gone now, struck by lightning. We refused to have electric when it was first offered. We thought it would spoil the atmosphere.

We brought our cabin from Billy Mitchell, the fish and chip shop man from Wednesbury, he was a character. I offered £180 and his eyes nearly popped out. £20 down and £10 a month. That was round 'Tin Pan Alley' (There were a lot of corrugated iron roofs). I built a new one on the same site though before I started, I rang the planning department, no one could give me an answer. One guy just said, "We don't want to know what goes on up there." I saw Dave the farmer and showed him where the stakes were in the ground, and he was fine about it. It had two gables and was by the tree with the swing for the kids. This is our third cabin although we moved off the site for a while before coming back."

53

Up on the Hill

The overall feeling from talking to the residents at Hill Farm is that they have an incredibly special sense of belonging. Residents tell of grandparents and great grandparents that first occupied their plot, building their bungalows themselves. They are absolutely attached to their plots, not surprisingly given the history of the place. Quite a few have other relatives living at the farm. Most live here permanently, working locally, many have children at schools nearby. There is talk of growing up here among the trees and the trains, the farm animals and the river. They talk of how their home here began, of what the original materials were, of where they were sourced and how they were transported. A pride that only comes with the satisfaction of understanding how every detail of their house came to be and from the battles that were fought to remain in it.

Barely two miles from the town but the place feels as remote a landscape as you might find in Wales or Cumbria. Crime is a rarity, you would need to be mad to think you could ever get away, there is only one road out and no turn offs whatsoever. Tales are told of those that tried and failed miserably! Local characters feature strongly in the reminisces of residents, fishermen, poachers, local businessmen, celebrities, and dignitaries, including one particularly prominent and colourful former M.P. A sense of discretion prevented me from going into detail.

On a beautiful sunny day there are few better vistas, although the winters up on the hill are brutal with roads impassable and services impossible. There is a hardiness to those that have endured many winters in this spot. There are the people and the animals, but the inescapable features of the landscape and its story are the railway and the river as they run together, timelessly through the valley.

Bibliography and Other Sources

Severn Heaven. Abroad in Britain, Jonathon Meades 1990.
Arcadia for All. Dennis Hardy and Colin Ward. Mansell 1984.
Plotlands of Shepperton. Stefan Szczelkun. Routine Art Co. 2020.
Humberstone Fitties: Story of a Lincolnshire Plotland. Alan Dowling. Cleethorpes 2001.
The Plotlands Museum. Essex. Essexwt.org.uk
Conservation areas, South Wales. WalesOnline.
Institute of Historic Buildings Conservation. Fiona Newton 2012.
Worcestershire District Council. Severn Valley Shack Survey 1951.
Worcestershire County Development Plan Shack Survey 1979.
Worcestershire Countryside Studies 1970.
Re Development of Basildon. Town and Country Planning 1973, W.G. Kington.
Beginning of Saltdean today. Wayback Machine, Internet Archive.